A Guide to
AMERICAN STATES

Kansas

THE SUNFLOWER STATE

MEDIA ENHANCED BOOKS
AV2
BY WEIGL
ADDED VALUE · AUDIO VISUAL

www.av2books.com

AV² provides enriched content that supplements and complements this book. Weigl's AV² books strive to create inspired learning and engage young minds in a total learning experience.

Your AV² Media Enhanced books come alive with...

Audio
Listen to sections of the book read aloud.

Key Words
Study vocabulary, and complete a matching word activity.

Video
Watch informative video clips.

Quizzes
Test your knowledge.

Embedded Weblinks
Gain additional information for research.

Slide Show
View images and captions, and prepare a presentation.

Try This!
Complete activities and hands-on experiments.

... and much, much more!

Go to www.av2books.com, and enter this book's unique code.

BOOK CODE

T283868

AV² by Weigl brings you media enhanced books that support active learning.

Published by AV² by Weigl
350 5th Avenue, 59th Floor
New York, NY 10118
Website: www.av2books.com   www.weigl.com

Library of Congress Cataloging-in-Publication Data

Nault, Jennifer.
 Kansas / Jennifer Nault.
   p. cm. -- (A guide to American states)
 Includes index.
 ISBN 978-1-61690-788-4 (hardcover : alk. paper) -- ISBN 978-1-61690-464-7 (online)
 1. Kansas--Juvenile literature. I. Title.
 F681.3.N385 2011
 978.1--dc23
                    2011018329

Printed in the United States of America in North Mankato, Minnesota

052011
WEP180511

Project Coordinator Jordan McGill
Art Director Terry Paulhus

Photo Credits
Every reasonable effort has been made to trace ownership and to obtain permission to reprint copyright material. The publishers would be pleased to have any errors or omissions brought to their attention so that they may be corrected in subsequent printings.

Weigl acknowledges Getty Images as its primary image supplier for this title.

Contents

With prime farmland, Kansas is one of the leading agricultural states.

Introduction

W hen, in the movie *The Wizard of Oz*, the character Dorothy said, "Toto, I've a feeling we're not in Kansas anymore," she was noticing how different her home state of Kansas was from the mythical land of Oz. She was missing the friendly comforts of Kansas. In addition to its charming people, the state boasts productive farms and businesses, varied geography with some striking scenery, and many reminders of its pioneer history.

Kansas has a colorful past, shaped by outlaws, radicals, settlers, and gold prospectors. American Indians had been living in what is now Kansas for centuries before the white settlers arrived. The settlers came in search of new opportunities along the frontier.

Sunflowers are numerous in Kansas. Their seeds are harvested for food and for the oil they contain.

Wichita, Kansas's largest city, is located on the Big and Little Arkansas rivers. The sculpture Keeper of the Plains was built in honor of the United States Bicentennial.

In the years leading up to the Civil War, Kansas was at the center of the nation's bitter conflict over slavery. In 1854 an act of Congress allowed the settlers of the Kansas Territory to decide for themselves whether to permit people to own slaves there. Groups both for and against slavery flooded the territory with new settlers, who often clashed violently. "Bleeding Kansas" became a battleground for the next few years. Kansas joined the Union as a non-slaveholding state in 1861.

Much of the history and culture of Kansas is linked to its early settlers. In the 1800s Kansas was a center of Western frontier life and was populated by **homesteaders** and outlaws.

In more recent times Kansas has become for many a place of peace and good fortune, with rolling fields of wheat and giant sunflowers stretching toward the sun. The state is blessed with ample farmland, good mineral resources, plenty of water, and a central location.

Where Is Kansas?

Roughly rectangular in shape, Kansas is surrounded by four states. Oklahoma lies to the south, Colorado to the west, Nebraska to the north, and Missouri to the east.

Kansas is often referred to as America's Heartland or Midway, U.S.A., because it lies in the geographic center of the United States mainland. It is located halfway between the East and West coasts and about midway between Canada to the north and Mexico to the south. Kansas is also used as the center point for all land surveys of North America.

Kansas is served by a large network of roads and railroads. With about 133,000 miles of roads and highways, Kansas has the fourth-largest public road system in the United States. Interstate 70 crosses Kansas in an east-west route. Interstates 335, 35, and 135 also run through the state. The Kansas Turnpike, a tollway, stretches for more than 200 miles along some of these roads.

Kansas is more rural than many other states. The United States has an average of about 87 people per square mile, but Kansas has only around 35.

The city of Wichita's role in aviation has earned it the nickname Air Capital of the World. Wichita manufactures large commercial airplanes as well as smaller private planes.

Amelia Earhart was born in Atchison in 1897. The pioneering aviator disappeared in 1937, somewhere in the central Pacific Ocean, while attempting to fly around the world.

Kansas is named after the Kansa, a group of American Indians who lived in what is now central Kansas. The word Kansa means "People of the South Wind."

Helium in commercially usable quantities was found for the first time in 1903 in the town of Dexter.

Kansas is the 15th largest state in the nation in total area.

Kansas also has many airports. In fact, Kansas has played an important role in **aviation** history. Kansas-born Amelia Earhart is known throughout the world as the first woman to fly a plane solo across the Atlantic Ocean. Other prominent Kansas pilots include William Purvis, Charles Wilson, and Clyde Cessna, who were among the early innovators of flight. Today several major manufacturers produce aircraft in Wichita. The city is a world leader in the production of aircraft for general aviation, and military aircraft also are built there. The city's Kansas Aviation Museum has many exhibits showcasing the state's history in designing and building airplanes.

Mapping Kansas

Kansas is about 400 miles long from east to west, and it is about 210 miles from north to south. The Missouri River forms part of its eastern border with the state of Missouri. The Kansas River runs through the northeastern part of the state, and the Arkansas River crosses southwestern Kansas.

Sites and Symbols

STATE SEAL
Kansas

STATE BIRD
Western Meadowlark

STATE FLOWER
Wild Native Sunflower

STATE FLAG
Kansas

STATE MAMMAL
American Buffalo

STATE TREE
Cottonwood

Nickname The Sunflower State

Motto *Ad Astra per Aspera*
(To the Stars Through Difficulties)

Song "Home on the Range," words by Brewster Higley and John A. Lomax and music by Dan Kelly

Entered the Union January 29, 1861, as the 34th state

Capital Topeka

Population (2010 Census) 2,853,118 Ranked 33rd state

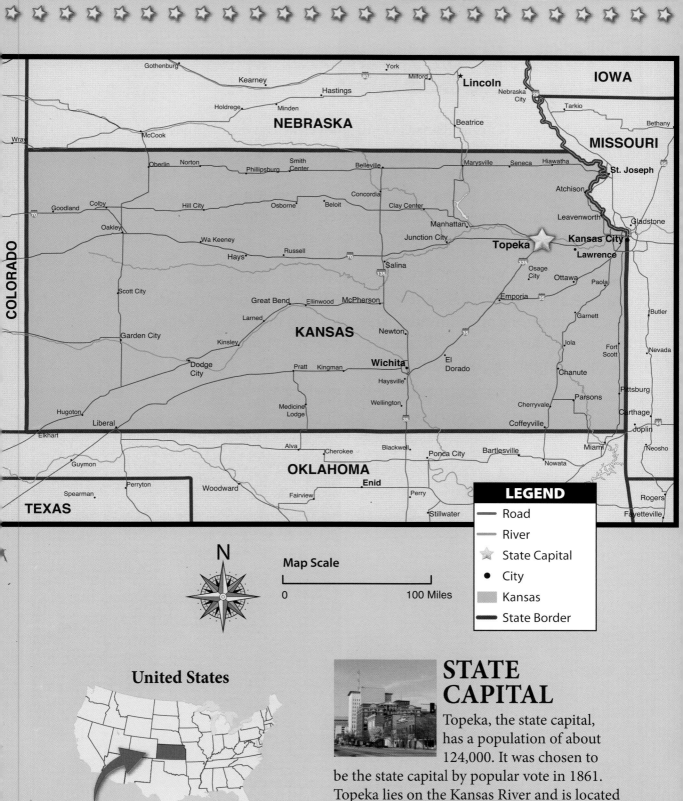

LEGEND

▬▬	Road
▬▬	River
⭐	State Capital
●	City
▨	Kansas
▬▬	State Border

N

Map Scale

0   100 Miles

United States

Kansas

Hawai'i   Alaska

STATE CAPITAL

Topeka, the state capital, has a population of about 124,000. It was chosen to be the state capital by popular vote in 1861. Topeka lies on the Kansas River and is located in the east-central part of the state. Agrculture, manufacturing, and government services are the mainstays of Topeka's economy.

The Land

Much of the land in Kansas is fairly level, with some ridges and rolling hills. Western Kansas is part of the Great Plains. The land rises gradually from the southeast, where the elevation is 780 feet in some places, to the west, where the elevation is more than 4,000 feet. The only large stretch of unplowed true prairie left in the nation is in the east-central part of Kansas.

The western part of Kansas has canyons and many striking rock formations. Because a large sea once covered Kansas, underground deposits of limestone are common. There are also many fossil beds, dating back millions of years. Kansas is graced by many sparkling rivers, including the Kansas and Arkansas rivers.

CASTLE ROCK

Gigantic cones of chalk tower over the plains at Castle Rock, south of Quinter.

PRAIRIE AT FLINT HILLS

The Flint Hills in east-central Kansas are the only large unplowed tract of true prairie left in the United States.

RICH FARMLAND

Kansas's **fertile** soil helps crops grow extremely well. Kansas has more than 65,000 farms covering more than 46 million acres.

CIMARRON RIVER

The Cimarron River runs through southwestern Kansas, before emptying into the Arkansas River. Many birds, including the cliff swallow, nest in the valley created by the river.

I DIDN'T KNOW THAT!

The rock formations at Mushroom Rock State Park were formed by water and wind **erosion**.

The Gypsum Hills were once called "Medicine Hills" for the river that flowed through them. The river contains magnesium sulfate, also known as Epsom salts, which aid human digestion and have other medicinal values as well.

Many lakes in Kansas were once strip mines. These mines were filled with freshwater and fish to create artificial lakes.

Kansas has one of the largest known **meteorites** on Earth of the type called pallasite. It is located in Greensburg and weighs more than 1,000 pounds.

Kansas is in a part of the North American plains called Tornado Alley, where tornadoes often occur. A tornado is a rapidly rotating column of air. It is visible either because it carries dust or debris or because there is condensed water vapor within the column.

Climate

O rdinarily, Kansas has warm summers and cold winters. The average July temperature in Topeka is about 78° Fahrenheit, and the average January temperature is about 28° F. Temperatures do not vary too much from one part of the state to another, but they can sometimes be extreme within a season.

The average annual amount of rainfall ranges from less than 20 inches in the west to more than 40 inches in the southeast. Kansas's skies occasionally unleash hail or blizzards, and tornadoes can occur.

Average Annual Precipitation Across Kansas

There can be great variation in precipitation among different cities in Kansas. What are some reasons for these differences in rainfall?

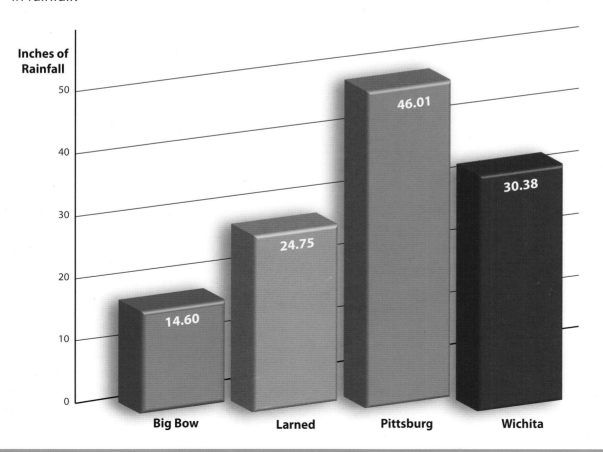

Natural Resources

The state's rich soil is good for growing crops. In the spring much of the land in Kansas is covered by fields of wheat. Most of the wheat grown in the state is a hardy, winter variety. It is planted in the fall and harvested in the early summer. Kansas is a leading state for production, storage, and export of wheat and sorghum grains. This industry has earned Kansas another nickname, the Wheat State. Other important crops grown in Kansas are hay, alfalfa, corn, soybeans, and sugar beets.

Wheat is the crop grown on much of the farmland in Kansas, which is known as both the Wheat State and the Breadbasket of the World.

Natural gas is extracted and brought to refineries, where it is converted into a product used a fuel. It is stored in huge storage tanks.

Kansas is rich in minerals, too. It produces large quantities of cement, crushed stone, clay, chalk, salt, and sand. Natural gas and oil are other important resources in the state. Most of Kansas's natural gas comes from a huge field in Hugoton. This reserve extends through several counties in southwestern Kansas, as well as parts of Oklahoma and Texas. Kansas also leads the nation in the production of helium, which is **extracted** from natural gas.

Kansas ranks seventh among all states in agricultural exports.

Cattle are raised on many Kansas ranches.

Wheat grown in Kansas makes up almost one-fifth of the nation's total wheat production.

Most of the state's harvested wheat is stored in concrete silos, but there are still some wooden elevators that date back to the 1800s.

The growing season in Kansas ranges from 150 to 200 days a year. This is the number of days in which Kansas crops can best be grown.

Plants

Many varieties of grass spring from the Kansas soil. Buffalo grass grows in the central and western regions, while bluegrass thrives in the east. Kansas is home to an array of wildflowers, such as Easter daisies, asters, clover, goldenrods, morning glories, and sunflowers. In fact, millions of sunflowers bloom in Kansas fields. Trees commonly found in the state include cottonwood, elm, oak, sycamore, ash, cedar, willow, and hickory.

Although the fertile land in Kansas supports many kinds of plants, the soil is constantly threatened by erosion. The constant force of wind and water puts unprotected soil at risk of being washed away or blown away. This problem has been partially solved by the improvement of farming practices and the planting of new trees.

GOLDENROD AND PRAIRIE GRASSES

Goldenrod and bluegrass grow in eastern Kansas. Bluegrass turns red in the autumn.

SUNFLOWERS

Sunflowers earned their name because of their tendency to twist on their stems to follow the sun throughout the day.

BEARDTONGUE

There are some 800 species of wildflowers in Kansas, including beardtongue.

COTTONWOOD TREES

Cottonwood trees grow freely in Kansas. They usually seek the damp ground along streams, rivers, and lakes. They have a lifespan of about 70 years.

The Tallgrass Prairie National Preserve was created in the Flint Hills region of Kansas in 1996 to protect an example of the once vast tallgrass ecosystem. Of the 400,000 square miles of tallgrass prairie that once covered the North American continent, less than 4 percent remains, primarily in the Flint Hills of Kansas.

Sunflowers are becoming an important source of **biofuel**, in addition to their use as a food source for both humans and animals.

In general, the prairie in the eastern part of the state is better for growing crops, while the Great Plains in the western part of the state are better for raising livestock.

Although most of Kansas's trees are deciduous, cedar trees grow in the northeastern part of the state.

Animals

Kansas is a place where the "deer and the antelope play," living up to the words of the state song, "Home on the Range." The open prairies provide a home for many different kinds of animals. Along with frisky prairie dogs, which burrow in underground homes, coyotes and bobcats live on the prairies. Other animals that roam Kansas include white-tailed deer, beavers, raccoons, skunks, opossums, and minks.

The survival of some animals has been threatened by overhunting. For many years deer had to be protected from hunters because the animals' numbers were shrinking. The deer population has since been replenished, and deer are no longer **endangered** in the state. The American bison, commonly known as the buffalo, has not been as fortunate. Bison once wandered the Kansas plains in great numbers, but they are now found mostly in protected parks and in zoos.

AMERICAN BUFFALO

The American bison, or buffalo, is Kansas's state mammal. A male buffalo can grow to weigh almost 2,000 pounds, while an adult female weighs about 700 pounds.

WHITE-TAILED DEER

White-tailed deer are very common in Kansas. They live in wooded areas and follow well-used trails to feeding grounds. White-tailed deer eat plants, and their diet changes according to the season.

COYOTE

Coyotes live on grasslands throughout Kansas. They are especially common along streams and in hilly areas.

RED-TAILED HAWK

The red-tailed hawk is found all year round in Kansas. It often perches on fence posts and utility poles along roads. Some hawks have a wingspan of more than five feet.

The Cheyenne Bottoms is a natural wetland area to which millions of birds migrate each spring and fall. These birds include pelicans, ducks, and whooping cranes.

Western Kansas has the largest population of prairie chickens, also know as grouse, in North America.

Hundreds of species of birds visit the Quivira National Wildlife Refuge, including the red-tailed hawk, bald eagle, and golden eagle.

In the late 1800s nearly 15 million sheep were brought into Kansas's central Great Plains from the Rocky Mountains to the west.

A world record was broken in 1998 when a fisher in Kansas caught a flathead catfish that weighed more than 123 pounds.

Tourism

Several interesting sites in Kansas offer reminders of its early pioneer history. On the Santa Fe Trail visitors can still find ruts made by wagons more than 100 years ago. Kansas is well known for its cattle drives, gunfighters, and dusty prairie towns. Fort Larned and Fort Scott have been restored, so visitors can experience some of the history of the Civil War firsthand.

Kansas has more than 100 lakes and 25 state parks. These parks include natural areas that are open to fishers, boaters, swimmers, and hikers. Another great way for tourists to appreciate the outdoors is on horseback. Trails for horseback rides through the sloping Flint Hills near Eureka allow people to roam the land as some early pioneers did.

EISENHOWER HOME 1898-1946

DWIGHT D. EISENHOWER LIBRARY AND MUSEUM

The Dwight D. Eisenhower Presidential Library and Museum is located in Abilene, where Eisenhower grew up. The site includes Eisenhower's boyhood home and a gravesite, where Eisenhower is buried.

SEDGWICK COUNTY ZOO

With almost half a million visitors a year, the Sedgwick County Zoo is Kansas's most popular tourist attraction. It is home to more than 400 different kinds of animals, including flamingoes.

MONUMENT ROCKS

Monument Rocks are a series of chalk formations that rise as high as 70 feet above the plains of western Kansas. They are also called the Chalk Pyramids.

KANSAS COSMOSPHERE AND SPACE CENTER

The Kansas Cosmosphere and Space Center in Hutchinson has the largest collection of Soviet space program memorabilia outside of Russia. Its collection of U.S. space program artifacts is second only to the Smithsonian Institution's.

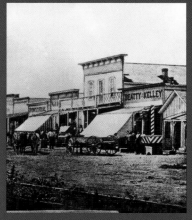

Abilene was the first Kansas cow town, and Dodge City was the last. Exhibits at the Boot Hill Museum tell the exciting story of Dodge City's Wild West beginnings.

The Topeka Zoo features more than 380 animals and includes a waterbird lagoon, black bear woods, and a children's zoo.

The National Orphan Train Complex in Concordia is devoted to telling the stories of orphaned children, mostly from northeastern cities, who were given homes by people in other parts of the country between 1854 and 1929. Many of these children found homes in Kansas.

Tourists may visit Cawker City to see an enormous ball of twine. More than 50 years old, it was begun in 1953.

Industry

Although most of the state's workforce is employed in the service or manufacturing sectors, farming and mining are still significant to the Kansas economy. The state's chief agricultural products include wheat, beef, and hogs. Much corn, sorghum grain, and hay are grown to feed livestock. The state's mining sector produces oil, natural gas, helium, salt, and materials for construction and for use in other industries.

Industries in Kansas
Value of Goods and Services in Millions of Dollars

Many different industries are important to the Kansas economy. Why might wholesale and retail trade be such a large industry?

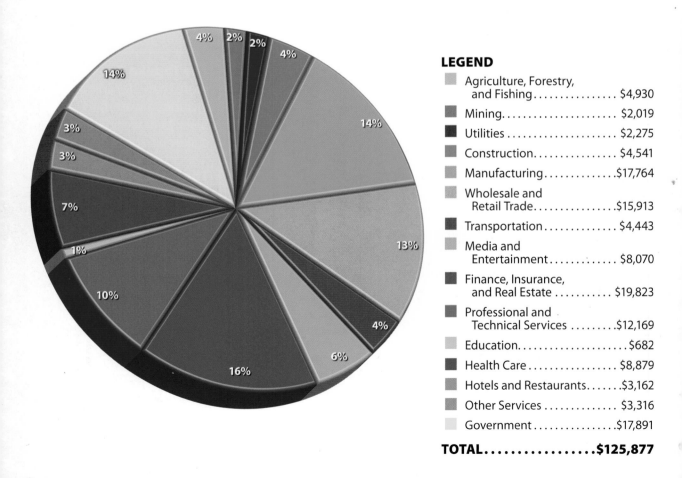

LEGEND

Agriculture, Forestry, and Fishing	$4,930
Mining	$2,019
Utilities	$2,275
Construction	$4,541
Manufacturing	$17,764
Wholesale and Retail Trade	$15,913
Transportation	$4,443
Media and Entertainment	$8,070
Finance, Insurance, and Real Estate	$19,823
Professional and Technical Services	$12,169
Education	$682
Health Care	$8,879
Hotels and Restaurants	$3,162
Other Services	$3,316
Government	$17,891
TOTAL	**$125,877**

Manufacturing is important in the state of Kansas. Items such as camping gear, heating and air-conditioning equipment, and snowmobiles are made in the state. There are several aircraft companies in Kansas including Boeing and Cessna. Publishing and printing are leading industries. Other products manufactured in Kansas are tires, paint, chemicals, industrial machinery, rubber, greeting cards, and clothing. Kansas factories also process the state's farm products and refine its oil. Many manufacturing firms are located in Wichita and Kansas City.

The Boeing Company in Wichita makes engines and other airplane parts. The state's manufacturing sector employs about four times as many workers as does agriculture.

The Stearman biplane was produced by Boeing in Wichita.

Wichita is a leading manufacturer of military aircraft, in addition to general aviation aircraft

Big Brutus, one of the world's biggest electric coal shovels, was used in Kansas in the 1960s and 1970s. Today it is preserved near the town of West Mineral by a museum dedicated to the state's mining heritage. Big Brutus is 160 feet high, which is taller than a 15-story building.

In 1915 an oil discovery close to El Dorado created an oil **boom** in the region.

Kansas salt mines produce salt that is used as a de-icing agent for roads, bridges, and other structures because of its low cost and ability to lower the freezing point of water.

Goods and Services

Kansas is a transportation leader in more ways than one. In addition to producing large numbers of airplanes and other transportation equipment, Kansas plays an important role in the movement of goods across the country. Because of the state's central location, most of the country has easy access to its rich agricultural output. Kansas has an extensive highway system. Kansas also moves goods in and out of the state by air and rail, as well as by barges on the Missouri River. The transportation industry employs a large number of Kansans.

Kansas's state highway system has been ranked third-best in the nation. The trucking industry in Kansas uses highways to deliver goods and transport products of many industries.

Located on the Arkansas River, Wichita contains both high-rise office buildings and parks. Wholesale and retail trade, government, and health care services are increasingly important to Wichita's economy.

Service industries, including transportation, employ most of the Kansas workforce. Many Kansans work in retail industries, such as automobile dealerships, groceries, and department stores. Other people work in restaurants and hotels, hospitals, law firms, wholesale trade, insurance agencies, banks, real estate, and government and the military.

Kansas has almost 70 newspapers and many radio and television stations. The state has six state universities, including Kansas State University, which has one of the country's leading agricultural colleges. The University of Kansas is located in Lawrence and has medical campuses in Kansas City and Wichita.

Two long-established Army posts in Kansas, Fort Leavenworth and Fort Riley, have contributed significantly to the state's economy in many ways.

The first newspaper in Kansas was the *Shawnee Sun*, printed in the Shawnee language. Jotham Meeker, a missionary, published it in 1834.

The Kansas State University College of Veterinary Medicine has a teaching hospital.

The Kansas Family and Children Trust Fund is dedicated to the prevention of child abuse and neglect. Kansas was the first state to establish such a fund.

The state has more than 140 airports open to public use. The busiest Kansas airport by far is in Wichita.

American Indians

Many different groups of American Indians were living in what is now Kansas when people of European descent first arrived in the area. Some of these groups included the Cheyenne, Pawnee, Osage, Kiowa, Wichita, Arapaho, and Kansa, or Kaw. The earliest people living in Kansas hunted bison and grew beans, corn, and squash.

The Cheyenne Indians were a farming people in Minnesota. When they acquired horses in the late 1700s, they moved south and west, changed their lifestyle, and became hunters on the Great Plains.

Several new groups of American Indians entered the area from the east after 1830. They moved into the region because settlers were moving westward from older settlements along the Atlantic coast, pushing American Indians off the land. The U.S. government began forcing American Indians to move west of the Mississippi River. Many wound up in Kansas. At the time, most American Indians had little control over where they were allowed to live.

Today, fewer than 30,000 American Indians live in the state. Some live on **reservations** in northeastern Kansas. The Haskell Indian Nations University was opened in 1884. In the summer American Indians from across North America meet in Kansas for **powwows**, which feature dancing and singing. Many American Indians attend powwows to renew old traditions and preserve their rich heritage.

The modern powwow is based on common values stressed in all American Indian cultures. These are honor, respect, tradition, and generosity.

The Spanish explorer Francisco Vázquez de Coronado traveled to the Kansas area in 1541. Coronado was accompanied by an American Indian guide and was looking for the legendary Seven Cities of Gold.

Explorers and Missionaries

In 1541 Spanish explorer Francisco Vázquez de Coronado became perhaps the first European to set foot in what is now Kansas. Leaving from Mexico, he entered the region on a quest to find riches that, according to rumors, were hidden in Kansas. He left the region after his search was unsuccessful. Juan de Padilla was a priest who was a member of Coronado's **expedition**. After his first visit to the region, he returned in 1542, hoping to bring Christianity to the American Indians. He founded the first mission in the area, north of what is now Wichita. Padilla was later killed by a group of Indians.

In 1682 the French explorer René-Robert Cavelier, sieur de La Salle, claimed a huge region that included what is now Kansas for Louis XIV, the king of France. This region became known as the Louisiana Territory. La Salle was the first European to travel the entire Mississippi River.

Timeline of Settlement

Early Exploration

1541 Francisco Vázquez de Coronado explores the Kansas region for Spain.

1542 Juan de Padilla founds a mission near present-day Wichita.

1682 René-Robert Cavelier, sieur de La Salle, claims Kansas for France.

U.S. Exploration

1803 The United States purchases the Louisiana Territory, including Kansas, from France.

1804 Lewis and Clark's expedition to explore the Louisiana Territory passes through Kansas.

1821 The Santa Fe Trail opens. This trade route, connecting Missouri with Santa Fe, New Mexico, crosses part of Kansas.

U.S. Territory

1830s–1854 The U.S. government includes present-day Kansas as part of the Indian Territory west of the Mississippi River.

1854 The Kansas-Nebraska Act establishes Kansas as a territory, allowing settlers to determine whether the future state would be slaveholding or would not allow slavery.

1854–1856 Kansas becomes a battleground for pro-slavery and anti-slavery settlers, including John Brown, who led a raid on pro-slavery forces in 1856.

Statehood

1861 Kansas becomes the 34th state.

1861–1865 Kansas fights in the Civil War as part of the Union.

1874 The introduction of hearty winter wheat helps make Kansas a major wheat-producing state.

Early Settlers

The U.S. government encouraged white settlers to move to Kansas. Government laws allowed them to buy land, even though American Indians already were living there. The government further encouraged settlement by refusing to force settlers off land when American Indians protested. As a result, the number of settlers moving to Kansas rapidly increased.

Map of Settlements and Resources in Early Kansas

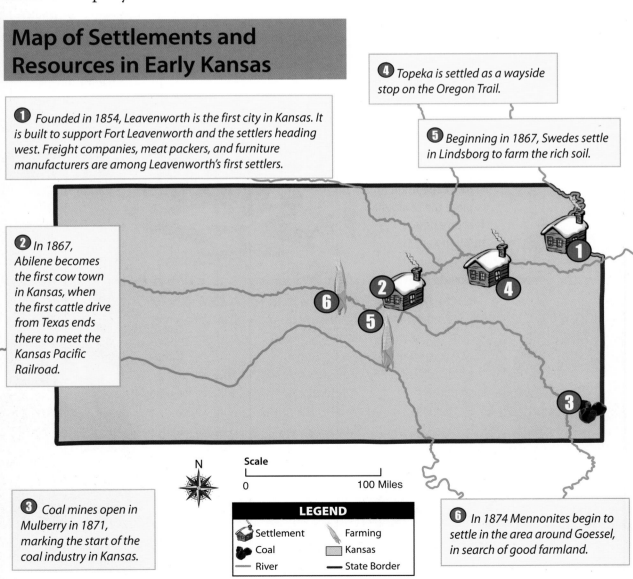

4 *Topeka is settled as a wayside stop on the Oregon Trail.*

1 *Founded in 1854, Leavenworth is the first city in Kansas. It is built to support Fort Leavenworth and the settlers heading west. Freight companies, meat packers, and furniture manufacturers are among Leavenworth's first settlers.*

5 *Beginning in 1867, Swedes settle in Lindsborg to farm the rich soil.*

2 *In 1867, Abilene becomes the first cow town in Kansas, when the first cattle drive from Texas ends there to meet the Kansas Pacific Railroad.*

3 *Coal mines open in Mulberry in 1871, marking the start of the coal industry in Kansas.*

6 *In 1874 Mennonites begin to settle in the area around Goessel, in search of good farmland.*

N

Scale

0   100 Miles

LEGEND

Settlement   Farming

Coal   Kansas

— River   — State Border

Many settlers moved into Kansas following the Kansas-Nebraska Act. Whether pro-slavery or anti-slavery, they came to farm the land. Towns such as Leavenworth, Topeka, Lawrence, and Atchison began to dot the prairies. Starting in the late 1860s, the coming of the railroad resulted in the formation of a string of cow towns along the railroad lines. Cattle ranchers brought their herds to these towns for shipment.

After the Civil War, former African American slaves settled in Kansas and began several communities. In addition, people from Europe came to Kansas looking for jobs, land, and adventure. German, Irish, and Swedish settlers all moved to Kansas. Mennonite settlers belonged to a religious group that followed a simple lifestyle of hard work and regular worship. Originally from Germany, many Mennonites went to Pennsylvania in the early 1700s to gain religious freedom. Later they expanded their communities into Kansas and other parts of what are now the Midwestern states. In 1874 Mennonites brought Turkey Red winter wheat to Kansas. This sturdy variety of wheat suited the climate in Kansas and helped give the state an edge in agriculture. The Turkey Red variety has become an important crop for many Kansas farmers.

Mennonites were known for their modest clothing and simple way of life. Like many Kansans, Mennonites believed in the importance of a caring community.

I DIDN'T KNOW THAT!

During the Civil War, rifles were smuggled into Kansas in boxes marked "Bibles" to avoid detection.

Laura Ingalls Wilder, the author of *Little House on the Prairie* and other books about her years growing up on the frontier, traveled in a covered wagon through Kansas. Her family stayed there for a short time in the late 1800s. More than 100 years later, the official *Little House on the Prairie* historic site was established near Independence. A small log cabin was reconstructed there, on the site of what is believed to have been the Ingalls family cabin described in the book.

In 1867 the Sisters of Charity opened the first Kansas orphanage, St. Vincent's Home.

The last American Indian raid in Kansas took place in 1878.

The Exodusters were freed African American slaves who moved to Kansas in groups after the Civil War. Their name is a clever combination of the words Exodus and dusters.

Notable People

Many notable Kansans have contributed to the development of their state and their country. One even became president of the United States. Other Kansans were political leaders, opposed discrimination in schools, or worked to improve life for all Americans. One Kansan became a nationally respected journalist championing the right of free speech.

CARRIE NATION
(1846–1911)

Carrie Nation spent much of her life in Kansas, where she was a leader of the **temperance** movement. She would enter saloons with a hatchet and smash the bottles and the bar fixtures. Nation was jailed many times, but her methods gained the country's attention. She was also a strong supporter of voting rights for women.

CHARLES CURTIS
(1860–1936)

Charles Curtis was born in Topeka. His mother was a Kansa Indian. He served in the U. S. House of Representatives and in the Senate, where he sponsored legislation to help American Indians. He also supported laws to help American farmers. From 1929 to 1933 he served as vice president of the United States.

DWIGHT DAVID EISENHOWER (1890–1969)

Dwight D. Eisenhower was born in Abilene to parents whose **ancestors** were Mennonites. During World War II, he became the supreme commander of the Allied forces in Europe, and he directed the invasion of Normandy on June 6, 1944, also known as D-Day. In 1952, Eisenhower was elected the 34th president of the United States. He served eight years as president.

BOB DOLE (1923–)

Robert Joseph Dole was born in Russell to a working-class family. After serving in the Kansas state legislature, he was elected to and served in the U. S. House of Representatives in the 1960s. He was a U. S. senator from 1969 to 1996. Dole ran for president of the United States in 1996 but was not elected.

LINDA BROWN (1943–)

As a third-grader in Topeka, Linda Brown had to travel miles to an all-black school. Her parents sued the Topeka Board of Education for unequal treatment. In 1954, in *Brown v. Board of Education*, the Supreme Court struck down **segregation** practices in schools across the country.

I DIDN'T KNOW THAT!

William Allen White (1868–1944) was born and died in Emporia, where he was the editor of the *Emporia Gazette*. His editorials were known for their mix of optimism and tolerance. White's editorial "To an Anxious Friend" defended free speech and won a Pulitzer Prize in 1923.

Nancy Landon Kassebaum (1932–) was born in Topeka and served in the U. S. Senate from 1978 to 1997. She was the first woman to be elected to the Senate who was not a widow taking her husband's seat. Kassebaum supported health care reform and fought for the end of racial discrimination in South Africa.

Population

Kansas has a small population, with about 2.85 million residents at the time of the 2010 U.S. Census. Of the total state population, about 13 percent lives in Wichita. Although Topeka is the state capital, its population ranks fourth among cities in the state. The largest cities in Kansas, in order, are Wichita, Overland Park, Kansas City, Topeka, Olathe, and Lawrence.

Kansas Population 1950–2010

Kansas's population has grown slowly since the middle of the 20th century. What are some possible reasons why the population has not grown more quickly?

Number of People

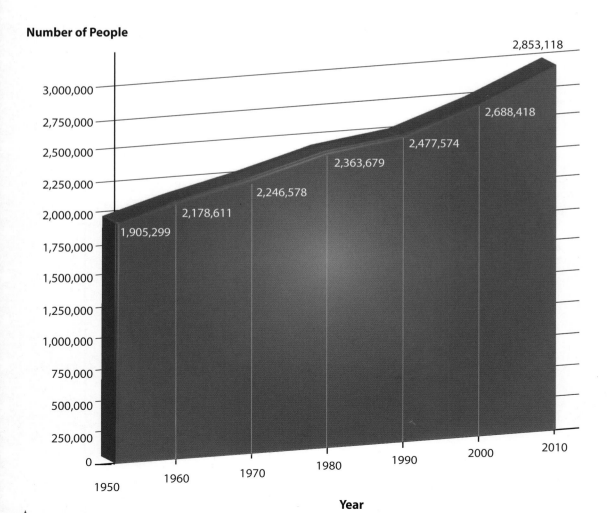

Year

Almost one-third of Kansas's people live in rural areas, where many families earn their living by farming.

Most of the early settlers who arrived in Kansas came from New England and were of European ancestry. Of the immigrants who arrived from Europe, most came from Germany, Scandinavia, Russia, and Great Britain. Today, the population of Kansas is becoming more diverse. About 6 percent of Kansas's total population is African American. About 9 percent is Hispanic.

Many African Americans in Kansas today live in and around the state's cities. In Kansas City, African Americans make up about 28 percent of the population.

American Indians make up about 1 percent of the Kansas population.

The largest city in Kansas, Wichita, has more than 372,000 residents.

None of Kansas's major cities are in the western part of the state. Garden City is the largest city in the west, and its population is less than 30,000 people.

Compared to the national average, fewer Kansans drop out of high school. About 86 percent of the state's residents 25 years old or older have earned a high school diploma.

The rural population in Kansas continues to decline. The poverty rate is higher in rural areas. Still, many people value the beauty and peacefulness of the state's rural communities.

Politics and Government

Like the other states in the Union, Kansas has three branches of government. The executive branch is led by the state governor. This branch makes sure that laws are carried out. The legislative branch is made up of a 40-member Senate and a 125-member House of Representatives and is responsible for making the laws. The judicial branch interprets the laws and governs the state's courts.

The state has been a leader in its treatment of women. Kansas granted women the right to own property in 1861. In 1887 women were given the right to vote in city elections. That same year Kansas elected the first female mayor in the United States. Susan Madora Salter became mayor of Argonia. Women won fully equal voting rights in Kansas in 1912.

The Kansas State Capitol Building was completed in 1903. It is made of brown sandstone from Shawnee County, and it boasts a copper dome.

Kansas was ahead of its time when, in 1861, it granted women the right to vote in school elections. Kansas women had to struggle for more widespread voting rights.

Kansas was involved in a landmark court case of the civil rights movement. In 1954 the U.S. Supreme Court ruled that the Topeka public school system could not have separate schools for white and black children. The court held that racial segregation in public schools went against the principles of the Constitution. As a result, segregation in schools in the United States was eventually brought to an end, allowing children of all races to learn together.

Kansas's state song is called "Home on the Range."

Here is an excerpt from the song:

Oh, give me a home where the buffalo roam,
Where the deer and the antelope play,
Where seldom is heard a discouraging word
And the skies are not cloudy all day.

Where the air is so pure, the zephyrs so free,
The breezes so balmy and light,
That I would not exchange my home on the range
For all of the cities so bright.

Chorus
Home, home on the range,
Where the deer and the antelope play;
Where seldom is heard a discouraging word
And the skies are not cloudy all day.

Cultural Groups

Most of the original white settlers who went to Kansas had already been living in the United States but were of European descent. Some of their descendants still celebrate their cultural traditions at festivals throughout the state.

Many people of Swedish descent live in Lindsborg, also known as Little Sweden. The city of Lindsborg has several festivals that feature some of the Swedish traditions of its citizens. Svensk Hyllningsfest is a festival that features traditional Swedish costumes, food, and folk dances and a lively parade. The first Svensk Hyllningsfest was thought to have started as a celebration of the landing of Swedes in America. Many Kansans enjoy learning about Swedish traditions and sampling their tasty foods.

Swedish people came to Kansas to have more opportunity to earn a living and practice their religion freely. Their love of music is one of the cultural traditions that has been passed down through the generations.

The Hispanic population in Kansas is increasing and contributing to the state's diverse cultures. About 14 percent of all public school children in Kansas are Hispanic.

African Americans have a long history in Kansas, beginning in the 1850s with the struggle over whether Kansas would be a slaveholding state. After the Civil War, many freed slaves moved to Kansas. Some African American soldiers who remained in the army after the Civil War were stationed at Fort Leavenworth. Their descendants settled in Kansas. African Americans who moved north during the Great Migration in the early 1900s often settled in and around Kansas City. In the Great Migration, many African Americans left rural areas in the Deep South looking for better job opportunities in other regions of the country.

In the early 21st century, the Hispanic population in Kansas has been growing. Around 9 percent of the state population is Hispanic. In some cities, such as Garden City, nearly half of the residents are Hispanic. The Kansas Hispanic & Latino Affairs Commission, a part of the governor's office, assists the state's Hispanic community and helps the state to celebrate National Hispanic Heritage Month every year.

I DIDN'T KNOW THAT!

The city of Wilson has a Czech festival each year, and the Czech Memorial Museum in Jennings displays exhibits about the region's Czech immigrants.

Many Scottish people settled in mining communities in the southeastern part of Kansas.

The annual Nicodemus Homecoming Emancipation Celebration has been observed continuously since 1878. African American descendants gather for a family reunion numbering up to 1,000 people.

The annual Polkafest in Hays features many polka bands, German food, and a Roman Catholic Mass with polka music.

Buffalo Soldiers were African American soldiers who remained in the army and were stationed in the Midwest after the Civil War.

Arts and Entertainment

Many rodeos are held in Kansas from spring through early fall. People can watch cowboys at a rodeo compete with each other at calf roping, bull riding, and barrel racing. The cowboys also ride bucking horses without saddles, trying to stay on the animals longer than any other competitor. In the steer-wrestling event, each cowboy tries to pin a full-grown steer to the ground in the shortest possible time.

Kansas also has several theaters, museums, fairs, and music festivals. The museums and other cultural offerings are mostly concentrated in larger cities, such as Wichita, and at universities and colleges. The University of Kansas has an outstanding museum of natural history and an art museum.

The state is known for its summer jazz and bluegrass festivals. People can attend bluegrass performances to hear this form of traditional folk music. Banjos are common in bluegrass music and are often played in an unusual, three-finger style. Bluegrass bands often include the mandolin and the fiddle. Attending a lively bluegrass festival will get even the shiest person dancing.

In addition to professional rodeos, several Kansas colleges and high schools stage rodeos. There are also youth rodeos at which children as young as five perform in various events.

Singer and songwriter Melissa Etheridge was born in Leavenworth in 1961. Etheridge has won several Grammy Awards, and she won an Academy Award in 2007 for her song "I Need to Wake Up."

Many well-known writers and poets came from Kansas. Gwendolyn Brooks was a poet who wrote about the African American experience. Damon Runyon, who was born in Manhattan, Kansas, wrote the hit musical *Guys and Dolls*. Independence-born playwright William Inge won a Pulitzer Prize for his play *Picnic* in 1953. He was one of the first dramatists to write about the quality of life in the small towns of the Midwest.

Kansas has also produced Hollywood actors and actresses. Kirstie Alley, Edward Asner, Dennis Hopper, Paul Rudd, and Don Johnson all hail from the Sunflower State. Hattie McDaniel, who was born in Wichita in 1895, was the first African American to win an Academy Award. She won the award for best supporting actress in 1940 for her role in the classic movie *Gone with the Wind*. Other Kansas-born artists and entertainers include painter Aaron Douglas, jazz saxophonist Charlie Parker, circus clown Emmett Kelly, and the founding members of the rock band Kansas.

I DIDN'T KNOW THAT!

Poet Langston Hughes grew up in Lawrence and went on to become one of the foremost interpreters of the African American experience.

Kansas actress Kirstie Alley appeared on the long-running television show *Cheers*.

People visit Lucas to view the sculptures of "The Garden of Eden." There, a local folk artist sculpted in concrete his own idea of paradise and other biblical stories.

Garden City claims to have the world's largest free concrete municipal swimming pool. The pool takes up half a city block and holds 2.5 million gallons of water.

The town of WaKeeney welcomes the Christmas season with an annual public tree-lighting ceremony. In a dazzling display, WaKeeney drapes its 40-foot Christmas tree with more than 6,000 lights.

Sports

Danny Manning is considered one of the greatest players in University of Kansas and college basketball history. He graduated from high school in Lawrence and left KU as the team's all-time leading scorer and rebounder after leading the Jayhawks to the 1988 NCAA men's championship.

While Kansas has no major professional sports teams, college sports are popular in the state. The inventor of basketball, James A. Naismith, was chairman of the physical education department at the University of Kansas at Lawrence from 1898 to 1937. He also coached the school's basketball team. Phog Allen took over for Naismith as the university's basketball coach. He was instrumental in making basketball an Olympic sport. For two years in the 1950s, the University of Kansas basketball team boasted Wilt Chamberlain as a player. As a professional basketball player, Chamberlain led the league in scoring for seven years in a row. In the 1961–1962 season he averaged 50.4 points per game and scored 100 points in one game.

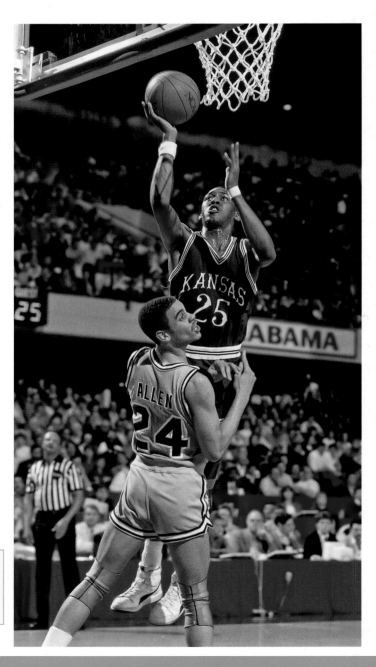

Danny Manning was inducted into the National Collegiate Basketball Hall of Fame in 2008. He works as an assistant coach for the Kansas Jayhawks, his former team.

The Kansas City Speedway hosts NASCAR events in June and October every year.

Wilt Chamberlain played basketball for the University of Kansas Jayhawks in the 1956–1957 and 1957–1958 seasons before he became one of the most successful players in the history of the National Basketball Association, or NBA.

In 1988 Wilt Chamberlain returned to Kansas to have his jersey officially retired.

Kansas resident Glen Cunningham held the world record in the one-mile run during the 1930s. His nickname was The Kansas Flyer.

Every summer Kansas hosts a challenging bicycling competition called the Death Ride. Cyclers ride 70 or more miles through heat, steep hills, and rough terrain over a two-day period.

Running clubs are a popular way for Kansans to enjoy the great outdoors.

Fans of auto racing can visit the Kansas Speedway, which opened in Kansas City in 2001. The 1.5-mile track hosts NASCAR and Indy Racing League races.

The state's parks and recreational areas attract many Kansas sports enthusiasts. The state has gained popularity among fishers for its many lakes. The state's fishing season is open year-round, so even non-Kansans can go there to fish when the fishing season in their home state is over.

Kansas has many trails for horseback riders, hikers, runners, and cyclists. Many of the trails in Kansas have sharp twists and turns. Kansas also has many parks for nature lovers. People can experience the fresh air and beautiful scenery of Kansas in these parks. Among some of the activities available to residents and visitors alike are camping, biking, and boating. With such a large number of wildflowers in the state, some people enjoy going on wildflower tours to spot, identify, and photograph the beautiful flowers native to Kansas.

National Averages Comparison

T he United States is a federal republic, consisting of fifty states and the District of Columbia. Alaska and Hawai'i are the only non-contiguous, or non-touching, states in the nation. Today, the United States of America is the third-largest country in the world in population. The United States Census Bureau takes a census, or count of all the people, every ten years. It also regularly collects other kinds of data about the population and the economy. How does Kansas compare to the national average?

Comparison Chart

United States 2010 Census Data *	USA	Kansas
Admission to Union	NA	January 29, 1861
Land Area (in square miles)	3,537,438.44	81,814.88
Population Total	308,745,538	2,853,118
Population Density (people per square mile)	87.28	34.87
Population Percentage Change (April 1, 2000, to April 1, 2010)	9.7%	6.1%
White Persons (percent)	72.4%	83.8%
Black Persons (percent)	12.6%	5.9%
American Indian and Alaska Native Persons (percent)	0.9%	1.0%
Asian Persons (percent)	4.8%	2.4%
Native Hawaiian and Other Pacific Islander Persons (percent)	0.2%	0.1%
Some Other Race (percent)	6.2%	3.9%
Persons Reporting Two or More Races (percent)	2.9%	3.0%
Persons of Hispanic or Latino Origin (percent)	16.3%	10.5%
Not of Hispanic or Latino Origin (percent)	83.7%	89.5%
Median Household Income	$52,029	$50,174
Percentage of People Age 25 or Over Who Have Graduated from High School	80.4%	86.0%

*All figures are based on the 2010 United States Census, with the exception of the last two items. Percentages may not add to 100 because of rounding.

How to Improve My Community

Strong communities make strong states. Think about what features are important in your community. What do you value? Education? Health? Forests? Safety? Beautiful spaces? Government works to help citizens create ideal living conditions that are fair to all by providing services in communities. Consider what changes you could make in your community. How would they improve your state as a whole? Using this concept web as a guide, write a report that outlines the features you think are most important in your community and what improvements could be made. A strong state needs strong communities.

What features make excellent communities and states? Consider features such as education, jobs, and social services. In an ideal state, what features do you think are most essential?

In what ways does your state meet your standards for an ideal state? What services does it provide your community?

In what ways could your state be improved to bring its living conditions closer to those of an ideal state? What services should be provided in your community?

2. Your State

1. Ideal State

3. Potential Improvements

How Would You Improve Your State?

5. Solutions

4. Obstacles

What are some solutions to the obstacles that you found?

What are some obstacles that could prevent the changes you outlined from being instituted?

Exercise Your Mind!

Think about these questions and then use your research skills to find the answers and learn more fascinating facts about Kansas. A teacher, librarian, or parent may be able to help you locate the best sources to use in your research.

1 What sugary snack was invented in Kansas?

2 Which legendary lawman kept the peace in Abilene in 1871 until he was fired for shooting at a group of rowdy cowboys and killing one of his own policemen?

4 Why is the city of Hutchinson famous?

5 Who invented the first patented helicopter?

5 Who was Carrie Nation, and what is she famous for?

6 How is the word Jayhawk connected to Kansas?

7 Why was Kansas known as Bleeding Kansas?

8 What was the Dust Bowl?

Words to Know

ancestors: relatives from earlier generations

aviation: the design, development, and production of aircraft

biofuel: fuel that is derived from plants

boom: period of rapid economic growth and prosperity

endangered: at risk of becoming extinct, or dying out completely

erosion: the wearing away of rock and soil by wind and water

expedition: a journey undertaken for exploration

extracted: removed from a substance by a chemical process

fertile: able to produce plentiful crops

homesteaders: people who settled on public land available for new settlement

meteorites: masses of stone or metal that have fallen to Earth from outer space

powwows: American Indian ceremonies

reservations: areas of land reserved for American Indians

segregation: the regulated separation of people of different races

temperance: the practice of drinking no alcohol

Index

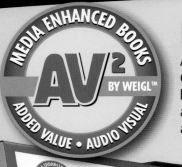

Log on to www.av2books.com

AV² by Weigl brings you media enhanced books that support active learning. Go to www.av2books.com, and enter the special code found on page 2 of this book. You will gain access to enriched and enhanced content that supplements and complements this book. Content includes video, audio, web links, quizzes, a slide show, and activities.

Audio
Listen to sections of the book read aloud.

Video
Watch informative video clips.

Embedded Weblinks
Gain additional information for research.

Try This!
Complete activities and hands-on experiments.

WHAT'S ONLINE?

Try This!	Embedded Weblinks	Video	EXTRA FEATURES
Test your knowledge of the state in a mapping activity.	Discover more attractions in Kansas.	Watch a video introduction to Kansas.	**Audio** Listen to sections of the book read aloud.
Find out more about precipitation in your city.	Learn more about the history of the state.	Watch a video about the features of the state.	
Plan what attractions you would like to visit in the state.	Learn the full lyrics of the state song.		**Key Words** Study vocabulary, and complete a matching word activity.
Learn more about the early natural resources of the state.			
Write a biography about a notable resident of Kansas.			**Slide Show** View images and captions, and prepare a presentation.
Complete an educational census activity.			**Quizzes** Test your knowledge.

AV² was built to bridge the gap between print and digital. We encourage you to tell us what you like and what you want to see in the future.

Sign up to be an AV² Ambassador at www.av2books.com/ambassador.